Wolfer's Primer

on

The Nature of Government

What they aren't teaching us but we need to know

Wolfer's Primer on The Nature of Government

ISBN- 978-1533645494
ISBN-10: 1533645493

prim·er

/ˈprīmər/   [prim-er or, esp. British, prahy-mer]

noun - derived from the Latin for primary.

1. any book of elementary principles

My promise:

**I'll work to describe just the key principles... those that
explain the heart of the subject matter concisely, and to show
where those principles come from. I'll stay away from too
much detail and avoid looking like an academic treatise larded
up with footnotes.**

Steve Wolfer

My other book is *"Wolfer's Primer on Progressivism"*

Contents

1 Introduction

When I'm learning about a subject, one of the first things I want is an overview of the entire subject – not detailed, because that gets in the way when what I want to know is what is being covered, and where are the boundaries. When I have seen the bird's eye view and know that I'm seeing the shape of the whole, then my learning is much faster and easier. Next, I want to know the most basic principles and the key properties of that subject. For me, these imply the approach, the scope and the format of the study material that I want, and that is how I've tried to make my primers.

Next, I want to feel that the author I'm reading doesn't have an agenda that is kept hidden. I want to know his or her bias or position on the subject. I want to know that when the writing is neutral on some topic, that it is because the author is neutral in that area. And that makes this the place where I openly state that my political beliefs coincide - more often than not - with the libertarian viewpoint. But, I expect to present enough facts and easily accessible observations so that readers will have no problem forming their own opinions and will be comfortable in knowing that I'm not hiding my position.

Finally, this primer is not an academic work and that is on purpose. I have no interest in expanding this work with endless footnotes or with a writing style that makes it suitable for the academic world.

Academia isn't my audience and that wouldn't be the kind of work I think our culture needs today. My purpose is to provide an approach to the subject of government that isn't arbitrary or subjective, that isn't a form of propaganda, or drenched with emotionalism.

Without basic arithmetic, neither algebra, geometry, nor any other math subject could be understood or used. Basic arithmetic is foundational. The nature of government is the foundational understanding needed to intelligently evaluate political positions, policies or ideologies.

I'm shooting for a small book that doesn't carry any unnecessary baggage, a book that respects the time and the intelligence of the reader.

2 The Basic Nature of Government

Government is a Man-made Entity

You, who are reading this, were born into a society where government already exists. Around the world, governments have existed in some form or another as far back as the beginning of recorded history. But despite the fact that governments have been around this long, we need to recognize that government is a man-made entity. It is not something that grows in the wild or something that pre-existed man's existence on earth. Any given government might be the result of purposeful design, or as an accident of history, or as some form of social evolution. But in any case, it is man-made, and it will continue to evolve under man's influence, and it will affect our lives, and it benefits us greatly to gain an understanding of what government is and what it should be.

Government Jurisdiction

As we will see, government is about rules, usually in the form of laws or regulations, and those rules are intended to apply over a specific geographical area. Even gang warfare is about 'turf' – about 'territory' – about who has the authority to set the rules for a specified area. The association of a set of government authorized rules with a specific geographical area is the basic meaning of jurisdiction.

Although government is always about territory, that isn't the only meaning for 'jurisdiction.' Jurisdiction can also refer to the subject matter or context. An example of this is when the United States ratified the 18th amendment to the Constitution prohibiting sale of alcoholic beverages (later repealed). The primary jurisdiction still applied (the geographical United States), but it was an extension of government rule-making to the importation, production, transport or sale of alcoholic beverages. This was the establishing of a new subject matter, a new context for government rule.

Jurisdiction can also refer to which level of government, which government agency within a level, and/or which court and/or which set of laws apply in a given situation. This makes it possible to eliminate competing and possibly conflicting rules by resolving this form of jurisdiction. For example, a question regarding the custody of a child would most likely be handled by the county's family court under the state's civil code.

Jurisdiction is the explicit or implicit declaration of the authority to enforce rules in a given geographical and subject-matter context.

Government's Stock in Trade is Force

A clothing store stocks clothes. Your grocery store stocks groceries. The stock in trade for your physician is a set of medical services. It is important to understand that for government it is force (or the threat of force.) Force, or the threat of force, is behind the military, the police, the regulations, the laws, and the court decisions.

Government has a Monopoly on the Rules for Using Force

By its nature, government has a monopoly on the legitimized, or justified, use of force. One limitation is jurisdiction. For a dictatorship the only recognized jurisdiction might be geographical. The dictator might not recognize any other restriction on his powers. When talking about the legal or political exercise of force it is important to distinguish between three kinds of force:

1. Self-defense which implies that some other party initiated the force being defended against,

2. Initiated force, which is always seen as unjustified, and

3. Retaliatory force, which is the force that government exercises against rule breakers.

Self-defense requires that force was initiated by another and that the defensive force is being exercised by the entity under attack or on behalf of the entity under attack by someone else. There is an immediacy involved. It is seen as preventative. Self-defense is not restricted to government, nor is it only exercised by non-government entities.

Retaliatory force is what we are referring to when we are talking about government authorized force. It might be an instance of a government authorized use of force to imprison a convicted rapist, or it might be a totalitarian government's use of force against someone who printed a news story the government disliked. To grant government a monopoly on the exercise of retaliatory force is saying that people should not engage in the private exercise of force for vengeance or engage in vigilantism. It is removing those forms of force out of private society.

The primary issue to understand regarding governments and force, is that a government is the only social entity that is "authorized" to set the rules about the use force.

Ayn Rand wrote, *"The difference between political power and any other kind of social "power," between a government and any private organization, is the fact that a government holds **a legal monopoly on the use of physical force**. This distinction is so important and so seldom recognized today that I must urge you to keep it in mind. Let me repeat it: **a government holds a legal monopoly on the use of physical force**.*

"No individual or private group or private organization has the legal power to initiate the use of physical force against other individuals or

groups and to compel them to act against their own voluntary choice. Only a government holds that power. The nature of governmental action is: *coercive *action. The nature of political power is: the power to force obedience under threat of physical injury—the threat of property expropriation, imprisonment, or death."

Government is a Social Entity

Imagine a person on an otherwise deserted island, they have no need for a government. Without a society - that is without more than one person - there is no need of a government. Evil governments consists of some kind of tyranny which makes its citizens victims to be preyed on. A good government is one that somehow facilitates the people living together, and flourishing, in peace.

Government can only Confiscate, Prohibit, or Direct Physical Force

These are the most basic capabilities of any government. It can prohibit, it can confiscate and it can direct physical force against individuals, organizations or other nations. Confiscate, prohibit and use physical force. It really can't do any more than that. Someone might say that it can provide benefits to people, but only if it first confiscates the funding needed to engage in giving. Government starts with only the power to threaten or use physical force and can only use that power to confiscate and prohibit.

> *Government is not reason, it is not eloquence—it is force! Like fire, it is a dangerous servant and a fearsome master.*
> ~~~~~~~ *George Washington*

Confiscation: Taxing, Borrowing, and Printing

Take confiscation for example: taxing is a direct form of confiscation; borrowing is a form of confiscation-once-removed because the loans and the interest will have to be paid back with future taxes. (It can print money or expand the money supply with central banks, but that will have the inflationary effect of diminishing the value of the money in existence, which is another form of confiscation.)

Government has nothing of its own. It has to confiscate from non-government sources to be able to hire government workers, fund programs, build buildings, wage wars or provide any aid. For example, before a government can provide foreign aid, or food stamps, or build a court house, it must collect funds from the private sector in some fashion – and rarely is the collection voluntary.

> *The American Republic will endure until the day Congress discovers that it can bribe the public with the public's money.* ~~~~~~ *Alexis de Tocqueville*

Wealth is created by private sector efforts producing something that is valued for more than its cost to produce. That extra value, that profit, is the source of wealth and it only comes into existence in the private marketplace. Government can take, but it can't produce.

Prohibiting

Prohibiting involves the creation and enforcement of laws and regulations that describe acts that people are not permitted to do. Sometimes these are obvious such as a law against armed robbery. Sometimes the prohibition is less obvious. Take for example the issuance of a marriage license. It appears on the face to be permission to get married, but what it should be seen as is a prohibition against getting married by all who can't meet the conditions that government sets down to get the license. For example, not applying for the license, not having a blood test if that is a requirement, not being of a certain age, etc. are all examples of legal conditions created by a government entity – conditions that if not met would make marriage illegal. When there is a marriage license requirement, it is government acting in the realm of marriage to prohibit some people from getting married.

Sometimes the laws might be stated as things people must do, like pay taxes. But that should be seen as a prohibition against people keeping their money instead of paying the specified taxes (and as a confiscation). Please note that I'm not, at least at this point, making a judgment about the value or necessity of any given prohibition or confiscation. Until we have a clear understanding of the nature of government, of what it is at its root, of what is fundamental to government, we aren't in a position to sort out what to do with government or what it should do with us.

Government is always about Force - not Choice

Let me repeat this. Government can only do three kinds of things: prohibit, confiscate and direct force at others. This is very significant in that all three are uses of force. The first two are threats of force. The most innocuous law or regulation and the tiniest of taxes are backed by the authorized use of a gun if the refusal to submit becomes an issue. This isn't intended as a condemnation, or a statement that all governments are tyrannies, but rather a statement that governments always deal with the "authorized" use of force which is diametrically different than say a friendship, or a free-market business transaction, or a private charitable donation, all of which are based upon choice rather than force or threat of force. In politics it is useful to keep in mind that basic dichotomy: Force or Choice.

Directed Force

Governments wage wars, and that usually presupposes confiscation of some sort to fund the war, and war is a very forceful form of prohibiting the enemy from acting on their own choices. The prosecution of a war, or the jailing or the executions of criminals are direct exercises of force. Confiscation and prohibition are actions backed by the threat of force.

Why Create Something Like This?

If, at their roots, governments can only direct force at people, confiscate people's things, and prohibit them from actions they might want to take, why would we want a government? Wouldn't it be better to not have something that can kill, maim or imprison us, take our stuff, and not let us do what we want? This gets to the heart of government by asking, "What is the purpose of government?" That is what is covered next.

We had to spell out the fundamental nature of a government before it made sense to discuss how it should be used.

3 The Purpose of Government

Government can be Evil

Clearly when we have an entity that is built to threaten and use physical force against people, we are talking about something that is terribly dangerous. In this sense it is like fire. There is a marked contrast between the fire we make our servant – such as at the stove to cook food or the fire in an internal combustion engine that powers our vehicles - when compared to a fire that burns down a house.

As we will see in the chapter on the history of government, there have been purposes that were not benign. Tyrants of all kinds have used government to serve purposes no good man would agree with. From history we have the examples of Stalin, Hitler, Mao, and Po Pot – just to name a few – that used government for evil purposes. So, a government, which is man-made, that can serve an evil purpose, is possible. What is needed is to define a proper form of government. And that requires us to define what the proper purpose of a government is.

*Concentrated power is not rendered harmless by the good
intentions of those who create it.* ~~~~~ *Milton Friedman*

Government is about Laws

Without going deeply into the nature of law or the forms it can take, let's say that the general mechanism of government is to declare and then enforce a set of laws over a given geographical area. Despite concrete expressions of a government, like a court house building, or a legislator, or a police officer, the government is an abstraction until it is clothed in a set of laws or edicts. It acts to carry out the law and in doing so it is those laws that make government a force in our life and not just an idea in our heads. Note that this is so regardless of whether we are discussing an ancient Greek city state, an Asian dictatorship, or the United States of America under its founding fathers.

Who does a Government Serve?

We can see at a glance that a dictatorship serves the dictator and his cronies. We can see through history that there have been governments that served some sort of ideology that was intended to bring about future benefits – realizable or not. This utopian approach to government is nearly always cast as a means of improving society – this is making society the beneficiary even if the appeal is to better the lot of this or that class of people. In effect the claim was, "Let us achieve this ideal form of society (in the future) and we will be better off."

In the United States, as it was founded, the beneficiary of the intended effects of government were the individuals – as individuals – and in the present as well as the future.

In this way we can see that the purpose of government has been defined by who benefits (whether there is an actual benefit that results or not). Is a proposed government given the purpose of serving society as a whole, or individuals who live in the society? Is a government's purpose, stated or not, the service of a ruling individual or elite group, or the citizens of the governed area?

Purpose Presupposes Moral Choice

To say or imply that government is man-made and that it has a purpose is also to imply that choices were made. That is to say, people made choices when writing laws, when advocating for this or that kind of government, when voting for a representative, or when participating in a coup or revolution. But this is only properly understood when our view of human nature is such that we believe that humans have some degree of choice. If we are instead creatures who can only react in pre-determined ways then any discussion of purpose takes on a different meaning. There is very little meaning left in word "purpose" for those who 'choose' to deny human choice. They will refer exclusively to the expression of genetic inheritance or to behavioral conditioning as the only explanation of human actions. But for the rest of us, who recognize that some degree of choice is a part of how we go about our lives, will have some form of a standard by which we choices are guided. What is good for us and what is bad for us? Moral choices are made according to some implicit or explicit moral standard. Is the standard for these choices based upon the individual as such, or is society somehow the measure of value? Notice that no matter who or what is to be the assigned beneficiary of 'good' and no matter what is the measure of 'good,' we will have accepted that government is to be purposeful in achieving 'good,' by some standard, for a given beneficiary. **In the realm of the man-made, one cannot escape 'purpose' and that implies choice and choice requires the existence of moral values.**

Human Nature is Foundational in the Purpose of Government

Without going into the details of human nature, let's stipulate that we are creatures who can imagine alternatives as we go through life. We cogitate on those alternatives with reason and/or emotions, and end up choosing between alternatives. There are many things that inform those choices: our belief systems, our values, our abilities, our habits, our character, our psychology, the situation in front of us, our capabilities, and our knowledge… to name some. But one that will be important in any society will be the laws of the land. Rare are the examples in history of societies that had laws but none of the laws effected the decisions of the people. The purpose of laws are to restrict or direct the choices people are able to act on.

Since government mostly prohibits and confiscates, the law will be about those activities. Tax laws, regulatory laws, and criminal laws will usually predominate, but there are many kinds of laws. For example, the latest whim of an insane dictator becomes the law of the land; the laws on voting in the old Soviet Union established a façade to cover the existence of only one party; and there are contract laws of a constitutional republic.

Whatever the laws are, they are means of expressing what the purpose of that government is. Needless to say, bad governments will generate bad laws.

So each government has its own purpose whether it is open and explicit, or hidden and even denied. And it is a proper job of those who turn a critical eye on the nature of government to measure the value of a government by examining the purpose of a government against what the purpose of a government ought to be. There are philosophers who will cringe at the sight of the word "ought" as if it were naïve to imagine that any form of moral yard stick can be applied to government's actions. But if one were to choose a simple standard such as a man's ability to flourish while being treated equally under the law as our yard stick we could go far in measuring one proposed purpose against another.

Government's Proper Purpose is to Maximize Individual Choice

For now, I'll simply say that the proper purpose of government is to minimize any and all actions that involve the initiation of force, the threat to initiate force, theft or fraud. The choice of that purpose over others becomes clear in the chapter on individual rights. For now, focus on the fact that a proper purpose for government is to prohibit only actions that reduce the ability of individuals to exercise their own choices and to do so by prohibiting those actions that involve force. The government in effect says, "To remove the use force, fraud and theft from the marketplace, government exercises prohibition, confiscation, and the direct exercise of force, but only to the minimal amount needed to defend choice." And the law that is proper to this kind of government will be only those laws needed to objectify that purpose. It is the separation of choice and force.

Clearly there are an almost unlimited number of kinds of governments that hold a purpose contrary to the protection of its citizens from force, fraud or theft.

It is because individuals can initiate force, or steal, that there should be laws that prohibit those things from the environment we all live in. At first glance it seems ironic to say that government is based solely upon the threat of force or the use of force while claiming that its proper purpose is to prevent the initiation of force or its threat. But it is the simple fact that humans make choices, and that they can choose to initiate force, or they can choose to live solely by free association and freedom of choice. Thus, we can see a society that permits the initiation of force and theft, or we can seek a society that bans those. And this is the crux of the issue: that we should separate choice and force. Government acquires a near monopoly on the use of force (excepting for self-defense) and thus removing it from all private actions. But this is a description of how government should be used: the proper purpose of government.

> *The ideal government of reflective men, from Aristotle onward, is one which lets the individual alone.*
> *~~~~~~ H. L. Mencken*

Ayn Rand has described the purpose of government like this: "*The only proper purpose of a government is to protect man's rights, which means: to protect him from physical violence. A proper government is only a policeman, acting as an agent of man's self-defense, and, as such, may resort to force only against those who start the use of force. The only proper functions of a government are: the police, to protect you from criminals; the army, to protect you from foreign invaders; and the courts, to protect your property and contracts from breach or fraud by others, to settle disputes by rational rules, according to objective law. But a government that initiates the employment of force against men who had forced no one, the employment of armed compulsion against disarmed victims, is a nightmare infernal machine designed to annihilate morality: such a government reverses its only moral purpose and switches from the role of protector to the role of man's deadliest enemy, from the role of policeman to the role of a criminal vested with the right to the wielding of violence against victims deprived of the right of self-defense. Such a government substitutes for morality the following rule of social conduct: you may do whatever you please to your neighbor, provided your gang is bigger than his."*

4 Individual Rights

If a person lived alone on an otherwise deserted island they would have no need for a government or its laws. There would be no purpose to having a government. Government becomes necessary when there is a possibility of conflict between people. Ayn Rand defines government as *"...an institution that holds the exclusive power to enforce certain rules of social conduct in a given geographical area."* She also says, *"If physical force is to be barred from social relationships, men need an institution charged with the task of protecting their rights under an objective code of rules. This is the task of a government—of a proper government—its basic task, its only moral justification and the reason why men do need a government."*

A right is any action that one can take without anyone's permission. Rand defines rights like this: *"A 'right' is a moral principle defining and sanctioning a man's freedom of action in a social context."* You should be able to carry on living, without needing to get someone's permission.

She believes that no one has a moral right to initiate force, threaten to initiate force, engage in theft or fraud. The reason those actions are singled out is that they constitute the only way to violate an individual's rights and it would make no sense to say that there was such a thing as a right to violate a right. Rights derive from the fact that humans must act to live, that we must be free to choose the acts we take, and this implies that there can be no such thing as a right to violate another's rights. And the only way rights can be violated is with the initiation of force, threat to initiate force, fraud or theft – because they violate our ability to choose.

For example, You should be able to use or dispose of your property without anyone's permission. For all actions that any person might take in a social context, you can say that they fall on one side or the other: actions one has a right to take, and all the rest are actions that you cannot take without some kind of permission.

There are no real conflicts since there can be no such thing as a right to violate a right. Under civil law, we have the means to resolve disagreements (determine who has the right in a given context) and therefore remove the need to exercise force in a civil/social context.

These rights arise out of the nature of human beings – out of our ability and our need to make choices as part of the process of how we go about our life.

We can see that the foundation of government is human nature, and that the standard that we derive from human nature is the concept of individual rights. As a standard it lets us determine what laws would be proper by asking what laws will support and protect individual rights.

So, if the purpose of government is maximize the ability of all individuals in the society to choose to take any actions that don't violate the rights of others (maximize liberty), then those rights become the foundation and standard for crafting laws. Government becomes for society what good security guards are for a company. They stay out of the way of the people, they treat everyone as equals under the rules, and they enforce only those rules that stop individuals from bad behaviors.

Volumes can be and have been written about the issue of freedom versus dictatorship, but, in essence, it comes down to a single question: do you consider it moral to treat men as sacrificial animals and to rule them by physical force?
~~~~~~~~~~ Ayn Rand

I want the people of America to be able to work less for the Government and more for themselves. I want them to have the rewards of their own industry. That is the chief meaning of freedom. Until we can re-establish a condition under which the earnings of the people can be kept by the people, we are bound to suffer a very distinct curtailment of our liberty.
~~~~~~~~~~~ Calvin Coolidge

5 "You didn't build that"

"You didn't build that," became a popular statement made by Progressives in explaining their belief that the successes seen in the business world were actually the product of the infrastructure that government provides. They mentioned public education, government funded research, the government funding responsible for the beginnings of the Internet, government funded roads and bridges, etc.

This immediately became a controversial statement, and one that is useful as an example of how to analyze a political position by referring to the fundamental nature of government.

The logical fallacy in this argument is that government couldn't have provided infrastructure, or anything else, without first confiscating from the private sector. Government can't produce from scratch. It can only confiscate and prohibit. Government funded research or government funded roads and bridges are all things that were funded by money taken from the private sector.

The private sector, on the other hand, can create products and services that are of value, and do so without government. Private roads and bridges and research funding are doable. What would happen if we went so far as to leave everything up to the private sector? What would happen if the private sector needed to provide police and military functions, for example? The absence of a proper government would require huge inefficiencies and costs in providing a defense against those who would initiate force, or engage in theft or fraud. Effective defense over an entire society requires a common set of understandable, enforceable rules prohibiting the initiation of force, fraud or theft. That takes us back to the purpose of government. Again, proper government isn't about providing 'infrastructure' but about removing initiated force from society.

The "You didn't build it," is an argument that attempts a back-door, false justification of having the government confiscate to provide all things by claiming the things are necessary and implying that only government can provide them and therefore high levels of confiscation are justified.

It also takes the choice of what to build, how to build it, and who can use it, away from private individuals and gives it to an elite in government.

This is an attempt that ignores the difference between those basic modes of social interaction: Force (or threat of force) versus freedom of choice. Government always is about force and the threat of force. The private sector is capable of existing with nothing but freedom of choice, i.e., an environment free of force – e.g., a government whose rules are about prohibiting the private use of force in society.

"You didn't build it," turns the issue of wealth creation upside down. By ignoring the fact that government can't do anything until there is some wealth it can confiscate, it can't create anything. It is the private sector interactions that generate wealth. Wealth is a product of human activity. If a government uses slave labor, it is confiscating that labor. That labor can create wealth, but the wealth will be less than would have been created had the slaves been free and able to choose their productive activities.

All of the arguments back and forth about "You didn't build it," will end up being about who gets to make the choice on spending. Progressives (and Marxists) will point at all the infrastructure used by entrepreneurs but ignore the fact that money was confiscated from the private sector to create that very same infrastructure. And their arguments will imply that there is no other way for infrastructure to be created. So, the argument they are making is that government will choose what to provide for society and how much of it to provide (and society will pay for it). The private sector will be arguing that they have exercised their choice, engaged in productive efforts and used what capital was left after taxes to build new wealth. Their argument is that the less the government takes, the more they will have available to create any infrastructure they actually need. The difference is, therefore, **who gets to choose how the money is spent: the people who earned the money, or the people in government who want to confiscate that money.**

The "You didn't build it," argument also highlights the difference in what should be a government's purpose. Progressives, Marxists, and others hold that the purpose of government is to make and enforce decisions that they claim will benefit society as a whole, even if it is at the expense of the individual. This purpose runs counter to individual rights. From this perspective, it is easy to see why progressives and Marxists will see property rights as subjective, and as limited or non-existent in order to act at the required level of confiscation implied by those who believe wealth and well-being are produced by government when it creates infrastructure.

6 The History of Government

Before there was such a thing as Government

This isn't a difficult concept to grasp. Imagine how animals live in the wild. Without the ability to conceptualize, much less to form contractual agreements, it is often brute force that rules. Those who can be eaten have to be wary and able to run, hide or fight off attacks. One can imagine that man, in his earliest of days lived in the same fashion. But with man there was the increased possibility of the concept of an agreement to not attack the other in exchange for not being attacked. There was some form of social evolution that was taking man from that brutal eat or be eaten law of the jungle to a de facto government where small groups stayed together to defend themselves.

What Forces caused the Evolution of Government?

Because man is conceptual by nature, and because man can transmit acquired knowledge to the next generation, there can be an purposeful evolution of sorts at work in the culture. This means that two forces are work at shaping government. The first is the far less purposeful and much more accidental byproduct of different social factions struggling with one another. With this we can see governments resulting from war and conquest and arms races and internal factions contending with each other. We can see governments grow more efficient, or just more brutal, as mechanisms used to prey on others.

But the other force is where men see what they believe would be a better system and they advocate for it, write about it, and teach the next generation about it. In that fashion, and to that degree, we end up with a government on purpose.

Government for all Individuals

The Declaration of Independence represents the first time a government was explicitly formed for the purpose of defending individual rights.

And the constitution became a written document purposefully set as the fundamental law of the land which described a government intended to be limited in its power and recognizing that the individual was the sovereign power.

Individual Rights Separate Force and Choice

When one can imagine the broad strokes of history relative to government what is seen is a progression towards increased choice. Government became the tool used to maximize the choice available to individuals. This cannot go far without an understanding of individual rights. And individual rights arise out of our nature as creatures who are capable of making choices.

All destructive forms of government will deny either that man has the ability to choose, or will make an attempt to justify inequalities under the law, or will deny that man is – by right - an end in himself.

> "Under a proper social system, a private individual is legally free to take any action he pleases (so long as he does not violate the rights of others), while a government official is bound by law in his every official act. A private individual may do anything except that which is legally forbidden; a government official may do nothing except that which is legally permitted.

> "This is the means of subordinating "might" to "right." This is the American concept of "a government of laws and not of men."
> . ~~~~~~~Ayn Rand

Recent history shows that the failure to observe constitutional limitations and the great increase in law - particularly regulatory laws, is inverting our system to where a private individual may only do what he is permitted by government while government can generate 'legal' excuses to do anything.

Of liberty I would say that, in the whole plenitude of its extent, it is unobstructed action according to our will.

But rightful liberty is unobstructed action according to our will within limits drawn around us by the equal rights of others.

I do not add 'within the limits of the law,' because law is often but the tyrant's will, and always so when it violates the right of an individual. ~~~~~~~ *Thomas Jefferson.*

What is true of every member of the society, individually, is true of them all collectively; since the rights of the whole can be no more than the sum of the rights of the individuals. ~~~~~~~ Thomas Jefferson.

Under the law of nature, all men are born free, every one comes into the world with a right to his own person, which includes the liberty of moving and using it at his own will. This is what is called personal liberty. ~~Thomas Jefferson

7 Democracy

Given that the goal of a proper government is the protection of all individuals' right to the pursuit of their happiness and to do so by the means of creating and enforcing rules that maximize choice and minimize force, what part can democracy play?

Clearly a majority vote can be as destructive of liberty and life as it could be a force for the good. Proof of this is seen in a majority that decides upon a lynching, or a majority that decides to enslave one group. Majority rule is a mechanism that can be used to resolve conflict and make decisions in a group or social setting. But like many mechanisms, it is neither good nor bad in itself. It is a means and not an end.

Those who advocate a system where the will of the people is put forth as the moral standard by which political decisions should be made or judged are not just wrong, but are often thinking of ways by which they can game the system, or just use it when they are part of a majority.

To the degree that democracy is unlimited is the degree that equality under the law is no longer possible and the system becomes like the three wolves and one lamb who vote on what to have for lunch.

Our founding fathers created a constitutional republic where the representatives are democratically elected, and democratically vote on laws, but all of their actions were intended to be strictly limited by the constitution. A vote should only be used where it can make a choice that can't violate an individual right.

8 Types of Governments

The best way to categorize government is through the essential characteristic of its purpose. Is that purpose to protect the individual citizen's right to make their own choices and to keep that which they own? Or is the purpose (openly, or deceptively) to provide some elite power over the individual citizens, their actions and property?

The next way to examine a government in terms of its type is to ask if the structure in question is effective in providing a stable protection of individual rights and in preventing the government from growing in power such that it would abuse individual rights. Or is the structure in question effective in keeping some elite in power and in confiscating wealth from the private citizens.

A Nation of Laws or Lawlessness:

If there are no laws, then the whims of the rulers will dictate the fate of the ruled. But very few nations today don't have laws since even those nations ruled by tyrants gain practical advantages from having a façade of laws.

Lawlessness obtains when the laws are so poorly constructed as to that they can't be understandable or when laws are impossible to follow or when laws are so many that nearly everything is illegal or when the enforcement of the laws is unequal, undependable or arbitrary. So, there are many ways that bad laws and/or bad enforcement is the same as lawlessness.

> *The more corrupt the State, the more numerous the laws.*
> ~~~~~~~~ *Tacitus*

> *It will be of little avail to the people, that the laws are made by men of their own choice, if the laws be so voluminous that they cannot be read, or so incoherent that they cannot be understood.* ~~~~~~~~~~~ *James Madison*

Representative Government:

Representative governments are referred to as republics. The idea is that the public vote to select individuals to represent them in making laws and/or administering the laws. The intent is to express the sovereignty of the people and to recognize a value in the mechanism of a democratic vote.

A key property of a republic is whether or not it is "constitutional." A constitutional republic should result in a government whose power is specifically defined and thereby limited, and whose structure is specified by the constitution. Note that there is a world of difference between a constitution that limits power as compared to one that doesn't, and a world of difference between a constitution that is observed and one that isn't. The former Soviet Union had a constitution that promised any number of rights, most of which were not actually rights, but rather promises to provide things taken from others, and little of which was promised was observed. It wasn't a real constitution, but rather a written lie.

Another difference is between those where the head of the executive branch is chosen by the people and is separate from the legislative body. This is a presidential republic. The alternative is where the head of executive branch is chosen in the legislative body – which would be a parliamentary republic.

Notice that a republic can have a monarch or not, and that if it does have a monarch the monarch's role can be largely ceremonial or the monarch could have real power.

A critical question to ask about a republic is if the representation is real, or just a façade - a rigged game. In the late Soviet Union people not only could vote for their representatives, but were required by law to vote. However, there was only one party – the Communist party – so the 'representation' was all façade. Prior to the American Revolution, the American colonies were subject to taxes mandated by the English parliament in which they had no representatives. The cry was, *"No taxation without representation!"*

Constitutional Government:

Governments are created by man, and run by men and there should be a written description of what the government's structure is and what powers it has. Such a document or set of documents is a written constitution. The constitution should be objectively written, understandable, the supreme law of that land, and provide specific limits to the government's power and jurisdiction. When it describes a government structure that is stable and where the constitution is taken seriously and not a façade, there is real benefit to the people. The alternative is a government without adequately defined limits on its power and/or no structure that provides stability over time. Real versus a façade is the question to ask where a constitution exists.

Democracy:

Voting is a way to make a decision where there are conflicting alternatives. A private club's members can vote on the club's rules. A vote can be taken by the people in a county to determine whether or not a bond issue passes to fund a public project for that county. Votes can be taken to elect local, state or federal representatives. Democracy is the use of voting to determine some aspect of government rule.

Unlimited democracy can be as evil and deadly as any form of tyranny – consider the actions of a lynch mob. The trick to democracy is to limit what majority rule can effect. If the vote on an issue would not violate an individual right, then voting might make sense as the best way to choose an outcome.

When a vote is used to pick representatives, that is not, strictly speaking, a democracy – not as form of government. That is a republic. A democracy would be like a small town that has a town meeting where every adult who lives in the town gets to vote on different issues. It is important to hold in mind this key difference between voting as a mechanism and democracy as the form of rule. Often we see communists, socialists, fascists and progressives treating "democracy" as a major political ideal instead of a mechanism. And usually this is done only where the vote is likely to move things their way, or where the vote is a façade and the real political decisions were made in other ways. Voting, too often, is a façade behind which an elite are manipulating and maneuvering the events. Democracy without individual rights is just another kind of tyranny.

Populism is the name of an ideology where the majority rule, e.g., popular rule is pushed out as the gold standard of what is politically right. In other words, if the majority votes for abusing the rights of a minority, it is okay. Populists won't own up to that, but it is an inescapable aspect of populism.

Nationalism and populism often go hand in hand. Often, nationalism is a form of emotionalism that is used to manipulate the population into supporting the goals of a ruling elite. Nationalism, on the national level, is often like what is seen on a local level when a demagogue stirs up mod sentiment to pursue foul purposes.

The Founding Fathers preferred a republic over direct democracy and feared a run-away democracy inflamed with popular passions and with the idea of a populace being seduced by demagogues. They saw one of the values of a Republic being in a tendency of people to want to elect intelligent, responsible people and those representatives would battle out differing positions as they voted for the different laws.

Another problem needs to be addressed that arises out of identity politics. Entire blocks of voters are treated as if they were of the same mind, had the same needs and the same beliefs just because they have the same skin color, or the same gender. When this type of political movement, like Progressivism or Marxism, is successful in employing this kind of voting, it makes it impossible for the resulting government to serve the purpose of protecting individual rights. Groups don't have rights beyond what each individual has…. Otherwise it would be acceptable for a group to attain a majority and vote to strip away all the rights of the individuals in the minority. Imagine three or four wolves in a meeting with a lamb and a vote is taken on what to have for lunch.

Democracy is the road to socialism.   ~~~~~~~   *Karl Marx*

Welfare State:

The welfare state began as way for existing governments to fight off what they saw as threats from socialists, communists, and unionists. The modern welfare state began in Germany under Otto Bismarck.

A welfare state is where a relatively free-market nation engages in a higher level of confiscation for the purpose of redistribution. There are various claims put forth as justification: That humans have an innate right to some products or services, like health care or education. This of course ignores the fact that the right of people to keep what is theirs is being violated by the government as they confiscate in order to give away. Other times it is the imposition of a moral claim that the neediness of some are valid claims to what others have. That to be poor or sick or needy is, as such, a moral claim against those who are not poor, sick or needy and that is the rationale for violating individual rights. Some people believe that is right for government to impose this moral belief on others with force. Some of those who take these positions do so to acquire power and control.

The result is a mixed economic/political system. Part capitalist and part socialist or fascist (many of the twentieth century fascist states were welfare states).

The key principles at work here are the diverting of a government from the purpose of protecting individual rights to violating them - from an environment free of threats of force to an environment where the government gets into the business of confiscating more than it needs for protecting rights.

And, it has the effect, as government actions nearly always do, of inhibiting any actions by the private marketplace to solve problems. Left to itself a free marketplace will find ways to create and support all of those things the people in that society value. A welfare state substitutes the values of the elite who design and operate the welfare systems for the values and choices of the citizens.

> *Government is the great fiction, through which everybody*
> *endeavors to live at the expense of everybody else.*
> ~~~~~~~~ *Frederic Bastiat*

Often, the concept of rights is seriously damaged by using language that suggests a set of non-existent rights. People don't have a right to things that have to be produced by others. To say otherwise is to sanction a kind of slavery. If someone says they have a right to health care, they are saying that doctors, nurses, and others are obligated to provide their services without having any choice in the matter.

Socialism:

Socialism is a political system based upon the teachings of Karl Marx. The key components are an extensive, centralized control over nearly all aspects of the economy and coupled with massive redistribution.

Socialists claim a scientific basis to their system, but it is actually an example of motivation by promise of a false utopia wrapped in academic jargon.

Progressivism can be seen as socialism-light. Progressive don't provide any concrete end to which they are 'progressing' but a logical examination of their direction and means and stated values show the logical and historical links to Marxist theories.

In Marxist terms, it is the 'means of production' that are 'owned by the people.' Social ownership, i.e., 'owned by the people' means a centralized elite hold control. The control might take the form of outright government ownership in an industry, or simply extensive regulation. Decisions are made by a centralized elite who claim to be acting on behalf of the people. There may or may not be a façade of democracy or of a republic in the government's form of structure.

Socialism comes in a variety of different forms (e.g., Fabian, Trotsky, Democratic, etc.) Examples of socialist governments include modern day Venezuela, Nicaragua, Argentina, Brazil.

Socialism is hostile to business and to capitalism. Socialism cannot co-exist with individual rights and is hostile towards the concept of private ownership and to private individuals making their own choices. As a political ideology, socialism is second only to some of the more rabid theocratic political movements, like the fundamental Islamic caliphates, in its religiosity. The Marxist is likely to be an atheist and opposed to Christianity or other organized religions, but that is only because the underlying drive is to replace other religions with the adoption of socialism as if it were the sole religion.

> *Socialism, ... confounds Government and society. And so, every time we object to a thing being done by Government, it concludes that we object to its being done at all. We disapprove of education by the State - then we are against education altogether. We object to a State religion - then we would have no religion at all. We object to an equality which is brought about by the State then we are against equality, etc., etc. They might as well accuse us of wishing men not to eat, because we object to the cultivation of corn by the State.*
> ~~~~~~~~~~~~~ *Frederic Bastiat*

> *All socialism is slavery. ... That which fundamentally distinguishes the slave is that he labors under coercion to satisfy another's desires.* ~~~~~~ *Herbert Spencer*

Democracy is indispensable to socialism.   ~~~~ *Vladimir Lenin*

Theocracy:

In a theocracy the head of the state is seen as both the leader of the religion and the head of the state. The state is seen as acting on behalf of a deity. The laws are drawn from the religion.

Historically we have seen struggles between secular and religious forces over control of the state (e.g., the struggle between Popes and Monarchs during the middle ages.) In ancient Egypt, the Pharaoh was seen as part god. There have been kings who were seen as the son of god. In modern Iran, the Ayatollah claims to express the will of Allah. Other varieties of theocracies include Sultanates, Caliphates and Emirates. Historically, there have been Christian theocracies as well.

Our founding fathers wisely saw that religion and government should never be mixed – that the state should never have the power to favor one religion over another. Their belief was that religion should be left as a private matter of individual choice.

A theocracy should be seen as another example of an elite exercising control over others. Individual rights are not recognized.

Monarchy:

A monarchy is a form of government associated with rule by royalty. Historically, royalty exercised near total control over all others and the leader of the royalty was the monarch and held absolute power. As king or queen, the monarch's word became law. Royalty is transmitted along blood lines.

Over time, the power of royalty was moderated until, in some cases, they have a position that is only ceremonial. Most monarchs today share the power of government with a legislative body. There may or may not be a constitution that limits the power of a monarchy.

The important issue is not whether there are individuals who are considered to be royalty, but rather whether that 'royal' status confers any claim to be able to violate the rights of individuals. Initially, a king might be thought to be the son of God and to have the absolute right to what he wished with his subjects. Individual rights were not recognized.

Anarchy:

Anarchy is the belief that there can more justice and stability without any kind of government. Many anarchists believe that a free marketplace will be able to handle a societies needs for protection of their rights. But without a single set of laws based upon the defense of individual rights, all that the market place would provide is competition that includes the use of force. **A truly free marketplace is free of the threat or use of initiated force.** It takes a proper government to get initiated force out of the marketplace. Therefore, a **free** marketplace cannot exist until there is proper government. So, anarchy is a floating abstraction – an idea that is untethered to reality – a fantasy. If you get rid of government, there will be no possibility of a free marketplace.

The other instance of anarchy is often visible in protests that involve violence. That kind of anarchist is more of a nihilist who wants to tear things down. They are often associated with socialist and communist movements. We often see anarchists in the violent riots that proceed a socialist or communist take-over. To the degree that this is purposeful behavior with some kind of theory behind it, the purpose usually is to provoke the established powers into being more and more brutal in hopes that it will repulse people who will then favor change. That's a sneaky form of intimidation by physical force.

As far as this book and its theme is concerned, anarchy is not a workable or proper substitute for government. It will not protect individual rights.

Communism:

Communism comes in a number of different forms, but they are all derivatives of Marxist theory. They all call for all things to be owned and controlled by the state and, often, everyone is an employee of the state. The fiction that is maintained is that this is actually ownership by the people, but that is propaganda.

One of the variants is the so-called "State Capitalism" visible in China and, to a lesser degree, in Cuba where they allow a minimal amount of private ownership of businesses. This is not real ownership, i.e., ownership by right, but rather by permission of the rulers.

The Marxist justification for prohibiting private ownership is that everything must be in service of the ideal where all things will be produced "From those according to their ability, [and provided] to those according to their needs."

Communism is Marxism applied all the way and is built upon a class structure view of economics, history, and the culture. It is a call for continual revolution. It is the self-avowed enemy of capitalism and free enterprise. What most people don't recognize is that communism, socialism and fascism all require the rulers transform and control the entire culture – not just the political and economic activities.

Federal or Federalism:

Federal or Federalism refer to a union or confederation of states or provinces. It is tighter joining than could be created by a treaty which joins separate entities but rarely creates a new entity. It is a loose kind of joining rather than the kind of joining where two or more businesses merge, and in doing so cease to be the businesses they once were. It is more like a partnership which creates a new entity but without doing away with the partners.

The United States of America was once a set of colonies. Separate colonies, each of which belonged to Great Britain. They united in a very loose way to rebel against Great Britain and win their independence. At that point, each colony became a separate state. And here the word 'state' is used to mean the same as 'nation.' They knew that none of them alone were strong enough to fend off nations like Great Britain, France or Spain in the event of another war. So they joined together, loosely, as a confederation (akin to an 'association') of states. The federal government created was very weak because at the time none of the states were willing to cede it much power. But after a few years it became obvious that the federation was too weak to last. This was the reason for the Constitutional Convention in Philadelphia where our current constitution was created. It left us with a stronger central government than before but the new constitution was only ratified by the states because they believed that their power was adequate to prevent federal abuses.

Federalism is a concept in American politics that recognizes that the states are partners who have granted some powers to the federal government while retaining other powers. It is seen as a means of restraining and blocking excessive federal power.

The United States is a constitutional, presidential, federal republic.

Fascism:

Fascism is an authoritarian form of government that is a close cousin to socialism. It is socialism that substitutes nationalism and populism for much of the Marxist rhetoric.

Usually, a fascist state will have a dictatorial head of government who will replace valid voting. The dictatorial head of state might be a strong man, or a military group.

Fascist leader(s) have the power to make any actions illegal and nearly always tend to grow more and more oppressive.

Fascism is known for its forcible suppression of any opposition. The tone and style of the government usually motivates with propaganda that attempt to unify support by demonizing others (by religion, by race, or by nationality). Like socialism it offers a utopian view, but it is often more mystical and about a future where the opposition is vanquished and everything is brought into alignment with the national goals.

The essential element to remember about fascism is that it creates an elite group that acquire control and power over others. It is totally incompatible with individual rights.

*The essence of fascism is to make laws forbidding everything
and then enforce them selectively against your enemies.*
~~~~~~~~ *John Lescroart*

Capitalism:

Capitalism is actually the name of an economic system as much as it is
the name of a political system. It is not the name of a type of
government but it is listed here because it requires a set of laws that
defend property rights. It is a system of freedom of association and free
enterprise and requires an absence of oppressive regulations or
excessive taxation. This means that Capitalism is incompatible with
socialism, communism, fascism, or any other authoritarian form of
government. It implies the need of a constitution that defines strong
limits for the government. It implies a set of laws that arise out of an
understanding of individual rights.

*A major source of objection to a free economy is precisely
that it ... gives people what they want instead of what a
particular group thinks they ought to want. Underlying most
arguments against the free market is a lack of belief in
freedom itself.* ~~~~~~~~~~ *Milton Friedman*

9 Government Structure

We are looking at a man-made institution that is intended to serve a purpose within society. One of the benefits of living in a society, instead of alone on a deserted island, is specialization. I doubt that anyone wants to live where they would have to be their own doctor, grow their own food, make their own clothes, build their own shelter, defend themselves from criminals and foreign invaders, and invent, manufacture and maintain all devices and machines they wanted. There are huge benefits to be reaped from specialization.

We have specialization in government. To be a government is to have laws, and for this there are usually legislative bodies. The laws must be created and administered. Government itself is an organization that must be managed and this means executives and workers. And there are specialists to judge the law and the application of the law, which gives rise to courts and judges, and police and soldiers to defend.

So, in broad strokes, we have division between the legislative, executive and judicial branches. But this wasn't done to reap advantages of specialization, but rather to divide power in ways that each branch would restrict the growth in power of the others. Our constitution prohibits the judicial branch from making law or administering it. The constitution prohibits the executive branch from making laws or acting as a judge or the law. And the legislative branch can make law, but not administer it. Each branch is limited in the powers they have.

Add to this the concept of federalism, where the states are able to act in restraining the power of the federal government. The founding fathers knew that each state government would be more responsive to their own citizens and that the citizens could use the states to keep the federal government in check.

Another check on government power is representative government. The founders were not fond of democracy when compared to a republic. They saw the local citizens choosing the wisest among them to go off and join with the other representatives to write and administer the laws. They saw the representatives as likely being wiser, on average than the average of the citizens that elected them.

Similar thinking was behind was behind the use of the electoral college in choosing the President. They saw the electoral votes being apportioned differently from the popular vote as a way of preserving the power of small states. The founders worried about the future bringing a demagogue who would sway the people and bring about a government that would destroy liberty instead of protecting it.

With the checks on power provided by the constitution, the division of power between the branches of government (executive, legislative and judicial), the power that remained with the states, the power of the people to elect the representatives, and the electoral college we have a structure that suits the purpose of a limited government, limited in power.

10 Benefits

When we act purposefully we are acting to gain and/or keep some value.

We've touched in a general way on the value of a government whose purpose and value is to keep the initiation of force out of society, but we can focus in more specifically.

Man can survive by himself, but he can gain enormous benefits from living in a social context. He can acquire far, far more knowledge than by himself. Only in a social context can there be traditions and educational institutions for transmitting one generation's knowledge to the next generation – building more and more knowledge and skill as time goes by. And each increase in our level of knowledge makes possible greater levels of success and well-being.

In a social context, specialization is possible and this raises the efficacy of our pursuits far beyond anything that could otherwise be possible. These skills are also transmitted from one generation to the next, growing with each generation. The medical profession is an example of specialization and the increase of knowledge generation by generation such that the poorest among us today can live a healthier life than either the richest king of old, or the smartest man alive but alone on an otherwise deserted island.

Then there are the joys that are possible in a social context. Human companionship, and specialization provides for the arts and for entertainment.

All of these benefits, to be enjoyed, may require that individuals approach differences between people with a degree of acceptance and toleration. Nothing will automatically create these benefits. For them to exist, be available, be secure and expand over time what is required is a set of rules – rules based upon individual rights and are enforced by a government such as to create that social environment free of initiated force.

There is also a benefit to living in a society where productivity, honesty, inventiveness, intelligence, and an openness to interactions are more the norm, as compared to living in a society where theft, threats, lies and fear are the dominate traits. Most societies are a mixture of the two and purposeful people should desire to move their society towards the first and away from the second.

11 Summary

"Government is a man-made social entity exercising the exclusive power of creating and enforcing certain rules of social conduct within a given geographical area."

That is a cumbersome definition of government but it highlights many of the key elements that are common to governments of all kinds.

- Government is man-made

- Being man-made, it is intended to serve a purpose (or a set of purposes). And purposes can be good or bad.

- Government is only needed where there is a society, as opposed to one man alone. It is a social entity.

- Governments are about enforcing rules. The rules of importance are the rules on the use of force. These rules could be the whims or edicts of a dictator or a military junta, or they could be the laws passed by an elected legislative body, or they could be the regulations created by an administrative agency of the government.

- To enforce rules implies the use of force or at least the threat of force.

- Government rules apply to a given geographical area.

Governments can only Prohibit, Confiscate and Exercise Force.

Rules by their nature, are usually prohibitions. Even a sales tax law, for example, (which is a kind of confiscation) can be seen as a prohibition against non-payment of the tax. In effect, a sales tax law is saying, *"All people are prohibited from engaging in the buying or selling of items unless those transactions include the calculation, collection, and payment to the government of a sales tax."*

A marriage license is a prohibition against getting married without first meeting all of the conditions specified by government as part of the marriage license law.

A Prohibition is a threat of force attached to a description of the actions being prohibited. And a proper government aims to reduce those things it prohibits till there is nothing prohibited but the initiation of force, the threat to initiate force, theft and fraud.

Government, by its nature, is about force. Like fire, it can be purposefully used in a beneficial way, or it can wreak havoc and destruction.

Force and choice are opposites. Choice is the natural mechanism directing human actions, but when force or the threat of force is introduced, choice is lost.

The heart of a government designed to maximize human survival and flourishing is one that creates an environment that maximizes the opportunity for people to choose…. To freely choose is to be free of force, threat of force, theft of fraud. This government would be one that only prohibits the initiation of force and nothing else.

If a society is to be free, its government has to be controlled.
~~~~~~~~~~~~~~~~ *Ayn Rand*

Beware of democracy for it is only a mechanism – not an ideal. A majority can decide to act in a way that harms the innocent. The measure of good government is the degree to which it is efficient in the protection of individual rights.

Governments come in many different types and can be structured differently. We have socialism, communism, theocracies, republics, democracies, constitutional governments, and on and on. But the essential issue will always be this: Is the purpose and effect of the government in question the protection of individual rights in a way that makes everyone equal before the law? Or, is it a mechanism for allowing the control of others by an elite.

Governments use confiscation, prohibition and directs force against people. It does so to suit a set of purposes. The most important thing to ask is, "Who benefits from any given purpose – all individuals, or an elite – all individuals, or some collective like 'public good' or 'society'?" Choice and force are like water and oil – and they just won't mix. If it is proper for man to be the one who makes choices, if that is freedom, if to make one's own choices is liberty, and if the propose of government is the protection of liberty, then the beneficiary is the individual, not a collective, and the measuring stick of success will be individual rights.

12 The Implications

If a proper government only deals with the protection of individual rights, how do all the other things get done? How do we take care of those who can't care for themselves? How are major roads, bridges, airports and other forms of infrastructure handled? How do we protect against pollution damaging the environment? Our government today does so many things, and regulates nearly everything which means lots of rethinking.

Understanding the proper role of government means understanding a completely different relationship between people and their government.

We don't just need to see government differently, but we also need to see our role as individuals and as private organizations differently. Each function that was provided by government, that was not part of protecting individual rights can become available as either a for-profit marketplace activity or as a private charity. The most important thing to keep in mind is that regular people are the ones who envision, invent, make the designs, do the engineering, make the decisions, and carry out the work. And this is so no matter if it was something done by government or done in the private sector.

Too often we forget that government isn't magic or from another planet. It is a group of our citizens working together to carry out projects and fulfill functions. And when these are done by government there is a considerable handicap that must be overcome. They must plan without the aid of information provided by the profit-loss functions of private enterprise and without the evolutionary benefits provided by competition.

In the private market, whether for-profit or a charity, the level of efficiency will be higher than if it is done by government. For example, given a chance, human ingenuity will find ways to build better roads, keep them in better repair, and the cost will be apportioned among us more fairly. And the overall costs will be less. These are simply some of the differences between done-by-government and done-by-private-enterprise.

It is true that some of the things that government does now wouldn't be picked up by private enterprise and some people wouldn't be happy about that. Some of them will be unhappy because they don't yet grasp the proper role of government and believe that there are things more important or appropriate than removing force from the social environment. Others will still be caught up in an angry or fearful partisan battle where having a controlling government feels necessary. But in a free market, things will be done if it they are wanted enough, by enough people. For some people, that will never be enough. They will feel that people have to be regulated for their own good and things that they disapprove of must be prohibited. There is no question that a higher level of tolerance is required in a free society. But the benefits a free society provides will greatly outweigh those disadvantages.

There are even people who want government to slow down the rush of technology and to force a slower pace of life. But this is actually an anxiety that the marketplace can help with... once the market is free enough. When the demand exists, the market will respond. Even if the product is a kind of cocooning from the pace of technology.

There is a great intellectual/emotional trap we fall into when we expect government to do anything (apart from protecting individual rights) for us, or for the poor, or for the oppressed, or for society or for the planet, or to create a utopia. These divert our minds and our energies away from reality and away from how we might find happiness and fulfillment in reality. Instead we become locked in antagonistic factions fighting to gain power over others so that we can make government make some magic that it never has been capable of..

ABOUT THE AUTHOR

Steve Wolfer has had several careers over the course of his life, and has stated that "psychologist" feels like the central aspect of his identity even though he isn't practicing now. He also created software for a long time – programming, designing and managing the software development process.

He left the family home in Wyoming as a rebellious 16 year old to live on his own and to travel. He was driven by a strong sense of adventure that may have come from how he felt as child when in the wilds of Wyoming's high country. This sense of adventure was later fed by deep water sailing. He sailed small boats in the Baltic, the North Sea, the English Channel, crossed the Atlantic single-handed in a 34 foot sailboat, through the Caribbean and the Bahamas, in the South Pacific and parts of Mexico. He confesses a love for travel to exotic countries.

His first heroes were men of the west – the last of the tough, old ranchers. Then he discovered philosophy from his father's Harvard five-foot shelf of books, going from the ancient Greek philosophers to Ayn Rand. After that his heroes were intellectuals and the world of ideas became the new lands to be explored.

He went from a high-school drop-out to a Master's degree in clinical psychology - interning under Nathaniel Branden to became a licensed psychotherapist. But above all else, his lifelong interest has been in learning. His passions are for those fundamental ideas that define our culture, our society, our political systems, and our motivations. Today, he lives in the Arizona desert, south of Phoenix and writes.

One Last Thing...

If you enjoyed this book or found it informative, I'd be grateful if you left a short review on Amazon. Your support does make a difference. I read every review and it helps me know what to change as I update the text, and it informs my thinking as I plan future books.

I have another book available on Amazon, *"Wolfer's Primer on Progressivism."*

Thanks again for your support.

Steve Wolfer